Praise for C.I. Aki

"C.I. Aki's *The World Black, Beautiful and Beast* is a bittersweet collection of poems that, like so much else from the south, nourishes us, in these most troubling of times."

–Lesley-Ann Brown, author of *Decolonial Daughter: Letters from a Black Woman to her European Son* (Repeater Books).

"Lyrically ferocious… Aki is not afraid to hold us to the fire, for it is where his poetic heart resides…[He] is a poet of deep feeling, clear vision, and vital honestly. We are blessed to hold his poems in our hands, hearts, and minds."

–Roberto Carlos Garcia, author of *[Elegies]* (Flower Song Press 2020), *black / Maybe: An Afro Lyric* (Willow Books 2018), *Melancolía* (Červena Barva Press 2016).

"Aki's book is an exploration of the self, and in the speaker's case, what it means to be Black in America right now. The poems are tender, bold, and inquisitive—often asking the questions many don't dare to ask, but should."

–Joanna C. Valente, *Luna Luna Magazine*

"The poems in *The World Black, Beautiful, and Beast* ignite our cultural thirst for clear-eyed justice amid the brutality of our history and our racist, violent present into rage, joy, beauty, and—ultimately—revolution."

–Katherine Indermaur

"C.I. Aki's beautiful new collection expands like a new vine into the cracks of the old monolith and utterly destroys it. An ode to the liminal spaces of a mind set upon by outrage, grief, longing, hope, pride, it challenges the credential of these visitors, and asks by what consequence we accept or reject them…[A] portrait of stars and stone…[This collection] is the sigh before the condemnation, the wistful smile before the Sisyphean trek, an elegant nod to the underbelly of *progress*, and the shortcomings of such blunt language. It is full of hope and beauty. Not a lament, it is the lasting song of lament."

–Maxwell Putnam

Publisher's Cataloguing-in-Publication Data

Aki, C.I.
    The world black, beautiful, and beast / written by C.I. Aki
    ISBN: 978-1-953932-03-7

1. Poetry: General 2. Poetry: Black & African American I. Title
II. Author

Library of Congress Control Number: 2021931262

THE WORLD BLACK, BEAUTIFUL, AND BEAST

C.I. Aki

Contents

To Desmond Coleman.

Don't let them erase you.

Contents

Will They Feed Their Eyes?

now awakened, will they
feed their eyes to see
what poems wander lost and blind
in the world that burns under this skin;
the world that burns under this skin
set afire by blue flames;
flames cooking a beaten heart that must house
and feed all that runs through its courtyards?

will they feed their eyes to see
what kind of words will leave
open scars on pages and realize themselves
in the name of a poem?

will they look? will they know?
will they follow the stories the skin keeps?
will it be written, spoken, or concluded –
all that the skin has read?
all that weary flesh the skin has carried?
all that original story the skin has written
with flesh and trembling?

will they feed their eyes to see?
will they desire to read the flesh
of the skin and the worlds it tells?
there are worlds it tells.
worlds.

The Problem of Pain (When it Doesn't Kill You)

Tell me where did you put all that fatigue and pain
I saw last night, trembling over your skin, and around
Your eyes and corners of your mouth,
When you couldn't stop crying and grabbing
At your shirt with your fist, after you heard
The news that they killed another one.
And this one was closer to you than the last one.
And the last time you saw them, tomorrow didn't
Sound like the dangerous lie that now howls
At every chance you try to close your eyes...
And return to those dreams that grow heavier
To keep alive; those dreams that grow heavier
To keep alive without the shelter of a promise
Or the security of a chance.

How do you now make your eyes appear wide
And fluent? After the confiscated horizons
And the tears that ran down those eyes
And out your nose with so much volume
And drain, with so much volume and drain
Your face swelled with the fear
That the heartbreak would never end
And the hole that was growing from the inside
Of your body would swallow your chest completely
Completely   completely
As you held the throbbing in your head

10

With those hands that first warned me
To stay away, to not touch you, or even speak
A single word.
Because all you felt for the moment, was everything
You could ever feel of the moment, falling apart, falling away,
Falling down, down, down a void too familiar, a vacuum
Too indifferent; pulling at your throat, snatching for your breath;
While the pain shook your body with revenge
For not finding a way to vanish or quit the arrest,
Despite the violent contradiction of its tantrums.

And do you mean it when you say, today
You will awake with eyes opened; you will awake with
Eyes opened once again, and you will step out,
You will step out, step out towards that same
World to find one of its eager days too ignorant
Of its crimes to hide behind the morning hours,
And you will stride once more, stride, beneath
The melting bronze of a squandering sun, striving, carrying
The only life you have this side of death, with passion
In your shoulders and waist, continuing, continuing,
Continuing, as if you haven't already known that
A surplus of threats, renewed and re-gathered, await you
Around countless corners?

11

The ~~Right~~ Fight to Be

It is my god-giving—yes, giving—right to fight
To stay right here—yes, here—and now, right
Here where I enjoy feeling the surge of sensuous
Circles of wind and fiction and truth strange
About me, moving playful, circling, kissing, and pushing
My face and side and feet, and calling me
                    to fly, to go, to go, to fly, to fly, to go—

But here and now—right here—where the cares face
The same tiring fears to have today—once again.
To wonder—once again,
If they will try—once again,
To end my fight chasing the call of the wind
                    to fly, to go, to go, to fly, to fly, to go—

Like them they ended
Who looked just like me.

Like them they ended
Who felt just like me.

Like them they ended
Who enjoyed about them
The same wind moving playful, circling, kissing, and pushing
Their faces, their sides, their feet, calling them
                              to fly, to go, to go, to fly, to go, to go,
to fly, to fly, to fly, to fly, to go, to go, to go, to go…

Before that tomorrow we all fear
Comes to take us away
With nothing to leave but a
Prayer that we don't stop
Fighting to stay.
Fighting to keep.
Fighting to breathe.
Fighting to be.
Fighting to be.
Fighting to be.
Fighting to be.

13

The Black Boy Joy

The black boy joy returns.
Even as the pain runs
Down the streets.
The black boy joy returns.
It cannot be stopped.
It cannot be justified.

It laughs the way winds on open hills laugh.
It lives the way winds on open hills live.
It cannot be stopped.
It continues, even after losing things;
Personal things; things that cannot return.
Things like people that cannot return.
Things that live and die with mulberry lips,
Strong Jaws, bent smiles, and eyes, eyes, eyes
Eyes bright and cooking like
Handfuls of fire keeping dreams,
Handfuls of fire keeping dreams
Of an endless dance after the same freedom
Caught up in the wings of birds,
Even after the broken wings,
Even after the added weight,
Lifting up falling skies like the hollyhock.

Yes, the black boy joy returns.
It cannot be stopped.
It cannot be justified.
It knows the weeping of things lost.
The weeping of losing things;
Personal things;
Things that cannot return.
Things like people that cannot return.
Things like people that cannot return
Who once shared that joy that
Cannot be stopped.

The black boy joy returns.
It cannot be stopped.
It cannot be justified.

Once There Was No Hope

Once there was no hope.
Only the embrace of an intimate myth
In song passed down before the exhaustion
Turned the last light into the next verse
Of that darkness never returned.

Someone told me that after George Floyd there can be no
Poetry. But how can I put into prose the howl of dying life?
The breathless bloodshed? The severed rose? The injury of injustice
Gnawing at my stomach and drowning the only heart I can carry
In the unanswered question of, *when will it end?*

When will it end? *When will it end?*
Will it ever change? How can I promise my daughter
More than she has survived? Is there a justice
That could ever come from a center so essentially maimed?
A center so essentially fixed?

Once there was no hope.
Only the promises of you and us, the breath of belief,
The warm touch of your earth, the way your eyes
Recalled the shine of fish scales under the sun
When you wept with me, or made love with me, or kept home with me,
Or fought them with me, or shared that same unanswered
Question with me, *when will it end?*

When will it end?
They killed Breonna in her freedom to sleep.
They killed Breonna in her freedom to find relief from that
Unanswered question. They killed Breonna in her freedom to dream
Beyond that unanswered question. *When will it end?*

What is language's parallel to that? How could I ever make that
Clear in words and lines that won't wander along the emotion
Of thought like old vines, or spread across the whole terrain
Of the aching heart like wild thyme in a deserted garden?

Once there was no hope.
Only the poetry of eyes climbing the length
Of long nights, as hour after hour fell on tired heads,
And in our weariness we laid our hopeless love
There under the warm weight of a simple desire,
With you wrapped in my arms, and me smelling the fatigue
On your skin, hearing words in your breath as you slept, words
Poetic and painful, sharing the presence of a promise not guaranteed
When we close our eyes, and find sleep, and relief, and dream
Of a world before the hope, before the burning
Unanswered question, before the inevitable rising walls of fire.

17

The Lady with Black Jaguars in Her Skin

Walking upon the falling night,
approaches the lady
with black jaguars
in her skin.

Her shoulders carry dissolving
moons on their crests
like hills watching at night.

Her stride is a blade;
a blade as sharp as
the silence she holds in her teeth.

*Come, let us hide together
and escape the empire that erases the world.*

How do you command the
slow, painful song of beautiful night
that winds along the contours
of your spotted flesh?

Where are the prophets who
delineate the seas that
stir at the bottom of your eyes?
The seas that keep watch
of your ebony bird
protecting your dagger.

Come, let us hide together;
escape the empire that erases the world.

Which ambiguities hide among
the humid fragrance your hair
makes of the night air, as
it climbs the penumbras of darkness
like plumes of the incense smoke?

Why do you leave me with this bouquet
of sorrow, coiling at my feet?
As you pass me by, leaving me
hopeless of ever knowing
the sanctuary of your maronages.

Take me, let us hide together
and escape the empire that erases the world.

Listen

A world of change.
Sometimes we call
It difference, some
Times we call it
Growth, some
Times we call it
loss.

Sometimes we
Wonder why it
Called us at
all.

And here we
Are. Called.
Answering
Calls. Calling
Out. Calling
out.

To Reading World

Holding this book, I take in hand
The first and last evidence that
We exists in lyric and faith
As truth torn and written, torn
And written by marks
Of praise and criticism, wondering
How it all survives the capture
Of thought, and desire, and
Knowledge, in forms of letters and
Phrases; truth without name, only faces
And description; all words and sentences;
A destiny in writing now given, now taken,
Now extended to feel between my fingers
Holding the grit of old dirt, flesh, and study of
The human story soiling the page.

I turn the pages, finding all these stories and words
And descriptions in more books that cover
My shelves, and my days, and my hours, and
My desires, with their stories
Facing me.

It was written to be held, marked,
Felt, carried, wondered, even read.

No Poetry in Privilege

"Censorship is the mother of metaphor." -Jorge Luis Borges

Why else did Plato banish the poets?
The same reason the imperial wears
White gloves and waves a flag of greatness
Cleansed of every question and temptation.
Because in his city, there is no such thing
As a slow dance, or the wonder if gods
Weep for the trampled iris, or the feeling
To set to flames a city that fails its
Least protected.

There is no poetry in privilege.
Privilege is allergy parading as hygiene.
Poetry is the beautiful contagion.
Privilege is the law of the private,
The law of depriving.
Laws don't write songs;
They write pledges, and
Ordinances, warning signs
And edicts: prescriptions
Of force.

The songs of the poem,
The songs of suffering the poem,
The suffering songs of the poem
Have never known the
Lips of power in the position
Of the subject, because the subject
In the position of the poem's
Suffering, is either rapture
Or the rapist.
And the suffering poem lies
In the bed of the patient, which
The Latin called passion, where no
Privilege is allowed, because
Privilege can't fathom the suffering of
The poem.
When it tries, it ends up with
Minstrel, or neo-liberal capitalism,
Diversity consultants, or the expensive
Insecurity of the academy.

And so the poem remains
The metaphor of a blessed rejection,
Building a secret city of weeping gods
Slow dancing with a trampled iris
Clinging to their hair, pressing their bodies
Together with the least protected,
Spreading a beautiful contagion
Against which, no law or vaccine
Shall prevail.
Plato be damned.

For the Children's Revolution Songs

Take these lines and put them at the end of the revolution
Songs the children sing, asking, with rushing eyes, why
The no's are louder than the maybe's and the yes's.

Maybe we can catch the break, before the clamor distorts
The next drop of the beat, with those lines of politicians
Selling justice, with hooks of hope upon the same lie about an arc
That bends only in the candidate's speech.
While the lie of an achievement gap betrays the speech
Of revolution children trembling with a future always lost;
A future always lost in translation of the teachers for America;
The teachers who cannot be teachers for a future that
Shapes a language beyond gaps;
A language beyond the gaps of oppression created by
Achievement of the old hands; the same old hands
Selling the old plans under the guise of new hands.

But the children don't believe it; you can see it in their eyes
Lost in songs about a world that keeps burning in their eyes.
Burning from a language that the folks call incorrect
Because they come from worlds unequal to the common core
Of the correct; the common core of the corrections,
That's why the children run for cover; they run for cover
From the correct, so their worlds can stay alive.

The children want a revolution. I can see it in the joy that
The folks want to improve, but the children run for cover.
They want their joy to stay alive; they want their worlds
To stay alive; they want their songs to stay alive.
Children, turn the music loud.

Black Not Allowed Genius

"The place in which I will fit will not exist until I make it."

-*James Baldwin*

Black not allowed
  genius or genus, only category
   of crippled, crying or
    colossal,
     when **Black** was the
     first to put Genius
      in motion put
       Emotion in genus (it)
       was Prez Young (you)
       sap suckers
        who slipped up
        and sounded
         the soundtrack
         of Cool you now
          google and claim
           as a code to be hip
      when the secret of Hip
      was the secret
       that Hip was the
       Secret of Blackness
       as Genius
       rejected
        rejection made
       Genius a
       secret as **Blackness** that
       sings…anyway

lives anyway
 dies anyway
  cause we all
   gotta die, but some
    know the Dance
     and some make
      the Songs
       of the secrets
        of Genius in
         the colors of **Black**.
          But **Black** not allowed genius.

The Sad Love Songs

what point should i make of justice,
if they say beauty and love are dead?
if I plan to drink to the oblivion of dancing,
why then must i wait on the coming
of noon?

there are red rooms filled with seductive
questions, playing music painful and pensive,
with corners of moving diagonal lights, sharing
lyrics you can sing but not explain, refrains
you can repeat but not remember. interested,
i wish to attend...

but I am being ushered to the white open scene
crowded with well-spoken gestures towards conclusions
and commonalities incommensurate of the mutual
and the deferring.
but it is said that everything is political;
therefore, i must follow.
but

what is the appeal of their imperatives on my behalf
if the eros of their desires is merely progressive?
why must i, *after all,* still have to jump on board—of their ships?
what distinguishes the imperative from the imperial?
why do they discourage me from lingering in thought and indecision?

28

where is my neither/nor? tired,
i wish to decline…

but i am being judged for keeping my time and my
scars, and my freedom, and my loves, in the dreams
of my flesh; the dreams of my flesh dressed in skin
and the urgency of history they compel me to write.
while the history of Being, they compel me to leave
to the work of old white men and their sons, as
their daughters review my submission with the
utmost scrutiny for clarity.

[to whom it may concern: i wish to stretch
these black hands and seize the authority of Being.
do you represent black authors of Being who
write more than *his*tory but the *whole*story
of Being? my story is semi-autobiographical. it
is set in a not-so-distant future, with a protagonist
caught under the final moments of crumbling arches.
ancient arches, weathered, beaten, rusted; the shape of
heaven's original distance, now surrendering a fetal
diastema not too scandalized to reach for the black
of my eyes. its embryonic principle of insufficient
reason draws my eyes upwards following the length
of each expiring leg, calling me, reaching for my eyes
to draw up, upwards; to trace the former supremacy made
trophic and entangled by the rendering of my dis-covering
taken to the point of succeeding the old, abstracted
measures of the vaunt and shape of those occluded heights.
now dis-covering the frayed veil of its incomprehension;

29

now surpassing the repeated measures of its unlimited loft;
now clapping eyes on the expensive vacancy of its darkened corners
protected from the broadcast of the sun's general light;
finally exposed to fertile eyes able to look the aging
terror in the face, with generational tears and dreams streaming down
announcing the words: i see images of men and women walking,
returning from the sun hand in hand. they look wounded and real,
and see how beautiful their strides strive *to be*.]
but

why am i judged as a rake for asking her to make it a double
after receiving another letter of rejection from them?
why is my style hardly legible and my eclecticism high-risk?
why do i have to fit in, and they are discovered to break ground?
why am i flowery, and they literary?
why is it hostile if i look my contradiction in the eye and say
you are not my equal, nor my counterpart, nor my ally despite
how many t-shirts and coffee mugs and yard-signs and reposts
you share with your lover and friends in those circles
you guard *now* declaring to all that my life
clearly matters since none of your lovers or friends
in those circles you guard at those tables you host,
passing brie and chic laughter, would find
your announcements redundant or sexy,
only political, merely correct,
merely relevant.
and so

i am judged for growing bored
of the talk, and the speeches, and the promises, and
the rage, and the voting, and the correctness, and
the corrections, and the censorships
of what is beauty, and song, and humanity, and existence,
and me.

The Crime of All Centuries

And what is the other side of our rough romance?
Is it a blanched, stiffened presentation, holding a sentiment by design
Away from the wilderness of the world eager to ravish its status
Of painted suns standing still, with hands of time that politely lie?

Our love carries stone-heavy desires of dream and beauty raised against
    high walls,
Wondering if centuries after, they will try to deconstruct these shameless
Passions as over-written prophesies about a strange thing called love. Or
Would they put the pieces back together to solve the crime of all centuries?

Their hate was a crime against the honest promise I held out to you without
Claim or demand, only the promise that my soul was prepared to risk loving
You, in a world prepared to hate every reason behind our freedom from
Hating love. We were a bond beyond bondage. Liberated from loving hate.

Until We Have Eyes

I wasn't born among mirrors.
I was facing fences, and windows,
And gazes, and wondering if I
Was the only one who thought
The audience had to be blind to be
So cruel and afraid;
All-knowing faces without eyes.

I spotted your large eyes from
The end of the room and dared
To comprehend the distance, but
The unsleeping sea between us turned over
Its ignorant whales and desperate sharks
And fell over itself in haste, like
Blind, furious, contradictions.
And I wonder now, how did we survive
The tempests, as the smell in your hair this
Evening reminds me of humid rainy
Evenings, and Spanish red wines,
And the way dusk pours
From intoxicated skies
The color of saffron.

How long can they continue
To slaughter the thinking and the dreaming by
A pulverizing premise too ferocious for desire?
A premise just as wishful as the dreaming, and
Full of sound, fury, and attention,
Eager to gouge out the eyes of the believers
So they can multiply the mirrors.

My eyes followed the vulnerability falling
From your skin that night,
Confession by confession,
Like the peeling bark of the crepe myrtle
At the end of a rainy summer.
We found ourselves
At the end of our rainy worlds, after
The beginning of our first kiss.
And the moon was laughing at our confidence,
Knowing history would find us delinquent.

But let's say nothing to the tyrants,
And those who could never believe that
The secret of living winks in the
Teeth of the lily blossoming at night,
While the lovers lock hands and
Write the best versions of their dreams
On flesh and bone and call it survival.

Tonight, let's make enough love together
Until the dawn finds us once again together.
Because I don't want to be alone when
The last metaphor dies,
And every symbol explodes,
And the world is finally corrected,
Fully defined and determined,
Savagely known
Without the need for eyes.

What is Soul?

What is Soul?
You and I lost in the rhythms
Of breath and flesh, feeling
All the feelings of the living
World without the desperation
Of the literal.

What is Soul?
What we think as we feel after
Words of the songs that get
Lost on our tongues becoming
One with the music.

What is Soul?
The reason we can dance upon fires and
Make wings of what is broken, with the
Plain pride of the plant insisting
To sway in the honey that must fall
From the sun.

What is Soul?
How we make love in the storm, and see
The beauty in the wounds of the words that
Write our stories of struggle and strength;
Stories of hearts bearing tremors; stories
Of risk and ruin, all that which was salvaged
From the sorrow turned to song.

What is Soul?
Still beholding from a distance,
Vague faces of rich color
Rubbing jaws that hold hymns
Too moving to be literal.

What is Soul?
That feeling of a certain evidence
We can only imply.
Asking ourselves, *Are we the last ones left alive in this world?*

They Said Black Superman Had to Die
(An Elegy to Curtis Mayfield and Them)

They said black superman had to die,
So all the King's men told his daughters.

He left his legacy somewhere on the corner,
Hoping we would make mythologies of it.
But we were told they were inappropriate
And would spoil our appetite for achievement.

He offered us sugar, honeysuckle, and a great big
Expression of happiness. All of which we learned
To call romantic and irresponsible to history.

He brought us a dozen roses and stories of righteous
Ways to go, every time he came from the big house.
But we learned his paradoxes were just hypocrisies
Made sweet, and the roses he cut had long been exposed,
And were already dying from lack of water.

He told us, we were second to none, even when
He returned to the big house. He tried to convince us
We were winners in a game he knew we already lost.
He knew we were blacker than blue, and so he called
Us Mother Nature's only god child, his sweet love child
In a world going to hell.

But black superman had to die. They said he
Was no good with the power. He was more famous
For being superfly than superman; although
He didn't find that as a contradiction.

He convinced us to speak a language he knew
Wasn't true, so we could have something to say
When they asked for the unexplainable.
He knew we would believe him if he told us to.
He believed that what made us true was not the truth,
But the joy of children laughing.

But black superman had to die. Because
When they came to arrest the music,
They said he was naked, drunk, and deaf to
The cries of his children. They said the sickness
He was hiding was eating away at his
Memory, and he was now highly contagious.
They said he let his boy grow up with a loaded gun
In his veins, and his pride wouldn't allow him
To look his daughter in the eye, when she tried
To name the monsters.
They said he used their mother to keep
The house in order. And when he disappeared one night,
With a woman younger and free,
Mother promised to never cry again.

So black superman had to die.
Along with his songs and myths of the train a-coming.
He wanted us to live on joy and laughter,
While the world turned his sweet exorcism
Into an outdated poison.

39

Words of the Fire Dance

Give me words of the fire dance.
The words with the syllables that pounce like
The blackest panther and slide
Like the quickest lie, or slightest truth.
Words that beat lines like Senghor's tom-tom
And dance upon the plentitude of meaning
Like Shange's letters, weaving fugitive language
Kept in turns of phrases lingering with allusion
And the belated shock of subversion.

Give me words of the fire dance.
Words with the inside eye of the Edo conceit,
Words that save language with renegade meanings
Of metaphors that extend and hopefully mix.

In the beginning was the word dancing in fire,
Calling all night from the end of a deserted street,
Promising to take us to the exact moment
When the Bird of Paradise flowers so
We can do more than just speak truth to power,
But speak power in truth with words of fire.

I want to write words that run on the page like
Rivers running at night.
I want to write words that travel the page like
Rivers running at night filled with water moccasins.
I want to write words that cover the page like
Rivers running at night filled with the mute
Music of moving water moccasins.

I want texture in words like tongues speaking in tongues,
Like tongues kissing tongues covered with songs;
Words that taste like the lisp of a long secret,
Or bite trochaic like my words when I stammer,
When I feel my breath caught up.
I want words that get me caught up;
I want words with mystery behind them.
Words like Magritte's play on the eye.
Give me words that call on the eyes
To taste the sound of the verses as they turn.
Words that hint—look!—Behind the lines
To find more meaning suggesting between a meaning
That is never still; a meaning trembling with promise
And instant fires. Evidence that clarity is a false intelligence.

Give me words of the fire dance.
Words carrying those melodies
Unheard of and said to be sweeter.
Words that soldiers stopped to hear
In the halls of their sergeant before
Swallowed by the slaughter.
Words that can lead us to the songs of love
Lost to the rule of law and clarity.
Words encoding the blueprints of revolutions and revolts.
Words that will dance with the fire.

When the Color of Black is Invisible
(The Black Dot That Was Not)

When I considered how my skin was spent on
The blinded gaze of threat or question, victim or fancy,
The black dot that was the not,
I remember that evening, when I was twelve,
And I was tired of the watchers and the keepers,
The ones who misunderstood, who mispronounced,
Who mistook, who missed me entirely.
I was twelve, and I was tired, and I felt
That I needed to close my eyes so
I could keep the tears from coming out
And the blinding world from coming in.
The black dot that was the not.

Back then my prayers were my poems, my confused reach
Towards the impossible that seemed unsayable.
Back then my poems were like quiet branches,
Skinny, bare, shaking,
But still somehow found by the wind;
Still somehow caught up with the wind.
The black dot that was the not.

I came to learn fiction before I learned truth, and soon
I learned love before I learned law. I learned to want the future
Before I feared the past, and I learned how to look in the face
Of loved ones taken by death long before
I heard the fresh cry of life, or the word daddy.
The black dot that was not.

Memories never leave, but desire can make a barefoot kid
Chase his dreams across the middle of a busy street,
Because he can't afford to wait for high lawns to run across,
And blinded gazes to select him based on well-earned merit.
The black dot that was not.

Today I tell Mikayla that eyes round can taste the sound
Of color and follow the song of skin. Today, I tell her
We were given these eyes to escape blindness,
And the categories of oppression, and history's lack of
Originality. Today, I tell her, the color that runs down your
Skin is as rich and certain as the blackest night keeping
Every star in its place; a flower of fire impossible
To miss by those who have eyes.
The black dot that was not them.

I

Never
To fit
In and
Follow
The loss
Of the
Wonder
Of how
Could
It be
That
We
Came
To
Exist
From
The void
Never
Gone
Now
Forever
Will know
Once
Existed
Was
I.

45

Being Demanded

"All you ever want to do is remind me I am black.
But, goddamn it, I also am." -John L. Williams

I am also the man who cried "I am." I am.
I am more than just a helper of history's
Passive speech. I am. I am more.
My soul draws more than only a mode of action.
I am an heir of all that could ever be. I am.

But how could I ever *just* be?
When being tends to linking, and linking
Seeks its complement, more so than
A compliment. I am.
I am who. I am what.
I am.
But how?

From the tangled noise into which
I stretch determined hands to
Gather names and descriptions,
Identities and styles, manners
And mistakes, do I find the
Sentences that I am after always
Terminated in the interrogative.
I am. But why?
Why am I?

Let me wander, and wonder if
I am here only essentially as a question
Marked by history, to question
Every mark on my history they gave
Against my quest to mark history,
My quest to mark history with this
Being of mine; this being of mine written
And not demanded; this being of mine written
Over all of their demands.
I demand I am.

The Sky is Falling

They say the sky is falling.
I don't see a cloud in the sky.
My ears hear promises of thunder,
But they lack lightning.

I must be blind.
I would rather be deaf.
I don't want to hear answers.
I want questions,

Like ask me why thorns
Bear the rose, or why living
Bodies fail hearts enlarged.
So I can recall the taste of

My tears, when the silent
Face of my mother, finally
Asleep to the pain, was covered by
The same rough ground she taught

Me to recall on rainy days
When all you have as cover
Is the whispering name
She would sing when I first

C.I. Aki

Learned those words,
"But honey *I* love you,"
Even when they use that word
I learned later to use as my word

But then I only carried loss
Of face, with pockets full of sand,
And still, the violet skies of dusk
Would pull at me, with their beliefs

That I could follow the birds that see
Beyond the fences surrounding me;
That I could turn circles in the sky
And kiss the briny lips of summer winds.

But all that started after she first said
"...*I* love you," with a mother's infinitive
Surpassing all tenses of time and mood
Making language pronounce my life as part of life.

My life as part of world,
As part of all.
Free to fly and free to fall.
Like they say of the sky.

This Beauty of Our Beast

It was when I spotted the tears gathering around your eyes,
Like clouds bearing a tenderness that endures with the patience
Of a stone sitting silent, silent under a restless sky dragging
Different clouds, grey and fat, with fits of rain desperate to fall upon
All that we had gathered from the confusion and war. It was
Then I knew our love would be a beautiful beast forever
Contested.

I wanted to promise only perfect things to your ears,
But a ferocious truth was always louder. I could never
Awaken you to a morning early enough to beat the
Sounding of the alarm. I waited for naked nights,
Black as ever, to show you analogies of our love.
On every chance I tried, a full moon appeared to dominate
The space.

And when I felt my shoulders wanting to curl over my chest,
Like a watchtower slowly falling to the sea from the terrors
Too many, the terrors too many to withstand and the waves that
Grew as our world quaked and pulled against us, and the
Desperate blindness, which surrounded, swelled. It was
Then I knew our love would be the beautiful beast forever
Contested.

I believe in the quiet religion of your embrace.
Your hands radiate with that special pulse of life that
Comes from three times the carrier of two hearts.
Let us carry together these hearts beating with life.
Let us carry together these hearts beating with life
Across the fields of contests, the fields contesting the
Beautiful beasts.

Breathe

Breathe.

The air between us has been
killed.

Breathe.

Let us gather ourselves,
Consider our words,
Clear our minds.

Breathe.

The chance of a new day
Awaits the fertility
Of a certain silence –
The potential of thought.

Breathe.

Everything's on fire.
All the exits
Are blocked.
It's only a matter of
Time.

Breathe.

I want to remember
The color in
Your eyes
And the taste
Of your promises
That helped me to
Breathe.

Breathe.

Elope the Gap

The pain is too great.
Too hard is the task.
Answers and reliefs
Of these losses will not be
Easy, nor popular.

Secrets are always
Hidden in the
Carefulness of listening.
What we desire will
Always wait for longer-
Eyes to elope the gap.

Life is harder than death (and)
Death's longer than life (yet)
Thought and love (are)
Stronger than both.
Why else exist these poems?

To You, Formally and Plural

and would i dare leave
an appeal so private, for
you to find in a text made
public, trusting that only
your manner of seeing could
pick out the quiet detail
waiting patiently, waiting
patiently to be collected
by your intelligence,
as its commitment to your
understanding runs the risk
of being discarded as meaningless?

and could i now admit to you
that all i ever had, were these words
that reveal their confidences after thought
and question, enduring on pages novel
and strange enough to dare
you to believe that they have
always been for you
and no one else?

Il N'Y A Pas De Hors-Texte

there is no outside-text.
all i have is right here.
all i could write, i write
here. right here as this
text.

there is no outside-text.
all i have is right here.
all i could write, i write
here. all that could escape,
i write here; all of it, right here;
right here as this text.
as a refuge of world, all of it
right here; as a refuge of me,
all of it right here, as a refuge
of text, all of it right here,
right here as this text.

there is no out-side text.

Only a Poem (Ars Poetica)

The hardest poem I ever wrote, was the lie I gave my daughter,
When her walnut eyes saw her mother's filled with tears, as
The chrysanthemums on the casket spray covered paw-paw's
Resting face, and she asked me will I die too, and I said never,
Not everyone dies, and the calm from my lying poem that
Covered her resting face, as she tucked her fear under my arm
Was worth the storm that started in my chest.

Ten years later I didn't die, but my comforting arm had to leave
Her resting face and walnut eyes, and the storm that I carried
For her since that day was obscured by the limit of the poem.

It was written, "Jesus wept," and *The Sound and Fury* ended
With "They endured." And between a weeping savior and
A remote last word, I see an anxious truth under
All of my poems, trying to shed its skin like a snake,
Because the rough ground it travels across
Carries bones and seeds. But unlike a snake,
It cannot shed its skin

When I am persuaded to use "we" in the poem
–making myself plural with you–
I am telling a lie I cannot outlive, no matter how much
Calm it promises to cover you and me from
The terrible questions we ask, when we see
Mother's eyes filled with tears, as the chrysanthemums on the

Casket spray cover paw-paw's resting face forever.
Had I only the strength to weep and believe, as my love
For you could never be remote, I would confess to you
The scandal that afforded my promise in every poem:
In truth, there is no "we," only a you and a me.
And these poems make this lie our earnest truth for the moment.
A lie, it cannot outlive to keep carrying earnest truth
From moment to moment. A lie, to protect you from
The ordinary truth of the moment; to make you feel safe
For the moment because it is too limited to make you feel strong
For every moment.

And so the poem, carrying obscure storms in its chest,
Pleads to offer you a moment; pleads to be forgiven for the limitation
Of its moments, pleads for the chance to try again after the promises break,
And the earnestness washes away, and the translucence of its skin
Reveals the truth of its limit as only a poem.

If

If there were a way to
Make dead hearts come alive
From laws passed, and countries
Healed by noble kings,
I would have told you to keep
Waiting for the morning's mercy
Like the watchman paid to count
The hours. Even though tomorrow
Comes regardless of him living
To collect his wages.

If there were a way to force the
Blind ones to see, and create equality
In spite of difference,
I would have told you to not
Call him back last night,
After the moment was interrupted
When they turned off the music,
And the lights chased away the darkness,
And the hands you used to bear his strangeness
No longer felt like a protection, or a love.
So he fled from the unmasking
That comes with that kind of recognition.

If there were a way to believe
A hope without intimacy,
Or an America without this pain,
I would have told you to dry your
Eyes, stop singing, love can wait
On our chance for justice,
And the attention is worth the ransom paid
Out by the masters' coffers to
Increase the volume of demand,
Despite how monstrous the means,
Or illusion.

The Fade to Black

"We surround democracy's false image in order to unsettle it.
Every time it tries to enclose us in a decision, we're undecided."
-Fred Moten & Stefano Harney

We know now, that the barbarians aren't coming,
And there is no reason why nothing is going on in the senate.

We know they turned the jungle into a zoo
And called their obsession for more, progress.

We know they wanted a better world view,
And so the world was taken out of their view.

We know they said the future was space,
And so they created a past of displacement.

We know they reversed separate but equal,
And then raised costs of equality.

(Terrorism of territory turned
Terror and territorialism.)

We know why the revolution is now televised
And why it can now make you look five pounds lighter.

We know why they are *just* anti-racist.
We know why we aren't friends.
I know why she gave me her office number.

Turn to the book of common prayer,
On the first right past the stadium.
Tell me if you can find a collect of hope in representation.

There is only church *in* the wild.
Only life and breath and death and bread, only
Dance and myth and sweat and love-making-love
Making-love and pain and pain and pain,
Because tomorrow comes only by chance
Of the rising sun, shining in the eyes
Of our young ones with hearts as small
And light as the buttons on their Sunday's best,
Listening to the old head cry out: "Everything
Is soul, be blessed, be blessed, everything is soul,
Be blessed. Make-with what you can
While there's little light to see, because
When it gets too bright to hide, we'll have to
Make that fade to black."

Because we know the barbarians aren't coming.
And there's no reason why nothing is going on in the senate.

Who is My Politician?

"Millions of black hands, across the furious skies of world war,
will be raised against their horror…the most disenfranchised of
all peoples will rise up from the field of ashes." -Suzanne Césaire

And while political and loud,
The signifiers of nothing buy up more clout
To the Capitol, to build up more capital
To survive the rout. And the roads aside
The loud and political, collect more
Victims of the rout.

I can hear the laughter in the dark; although they say
It's true remorse; and even be it true remorse, heard
From the darkness this long it all sounds like laughter.

Don't say my name after I'm dead, if you never
Said it when I was alive; if you never said it when
I was alive with life dreaming for a chance I made
Into music to pass the time I put together, the
Little time I put together from a rundown history
Now interrupted by you and those you could've stopped.
Don't say my name then.

I will not vote for you because you cannot vote for me.
You will not represent me because I cannot represent you.

Instead, I will save my hands and legs to bandage these wounds
And pour this oil and wine over scars reopened continuously.

I will walk down that darkened road, carrying my brother and sister,
Until I find that familiar innkeeper and tell her with my own voice,
To take this last dime of mine, and please watch after my brother
And sister. I'll return with more last dimes of mine, and more of my
Brothers and sisters.

We – our only chance of justice – don't ask for a ballot,
Only ask with the question, do you feel what I'm saying?

If you can feel what I'm saying, then we speak the same language.
If we can speak the same language, we can face the rout together.

Black Jesus Never Coming (Re: W.B. Yeats)

Luke 2:7

Returning, returning, the calls of hope,
For the achievement of giants to desegregate the space.
What crumbles aside their feet they call gaps, what underneath, realism.
    And the center stays the same. Space only changes its names.

Giants desire the volume. From afar, the ground is hard to see.
Precisely where they walk, they cannot understand. Therefore
The ceremony of knowledge and morality must abscond the thinking.
    While the loudest tongues lack no conviction. And
    The justice of passionate intentionality is loosed,
    And everywhere.

Surely now the giants will answer.
Surely now their answers will be giant. For if not,
Surely now they must know that another revolution
Will be at hand! Again for giant answers!
Again for the giants to answer!
    But no sooner the return of the evolution of that surety than
    Are we in need of a new call, a new hope, a new again.

A new vastness for achievement. A new possibility. A new technology.
With a form always amorphous. No head and all face. Entirely tongue.
    To resolve the deficit with pity and incomprehension.
    Dark and empty.
    The most sudden of all shadows.

And now louder the calls. Evoking feet busy with large steps
Besides which the gaps still reel. While all about the ground underneath,
The realism retains a specular confusion.
    A loud confusion of call, and hope, and mirrors.
    And the blackness vexes again. But now

I know that a witness 400 couldn't call the stony sleep slumber,
Or potential. Never the nightmare the cradle could rock away,
Even by the hands of giants.
    For the rough beasts have devoured all the public spaces
    With an increasing volume of indignation, hope, and *media res*.
    Returning and returning. Gaps and Realism.
    The space giants re-form to stay Time.

Meanwhile, watching their flock at night in low country, poor shepherds
fashion gospels out of free stars. Fabricating the folklore of a future
no room will ever furnish. And meanly wrapped, ever in infancy, cries
prophetic. *Vagitanus!*

The Secret Life of Growth

No one sees the secret life of plants
Producing their own future of life,
Like Spinoza's prophet of light
Describing only what the gods
Reflect, when the stars spread
Questions across the night.

The secret life of growth cloaks
That intimate secretion of life, as only
The incessant "but I must" repeated
And repeated. "But I must" repeated.
(A silent devotion unheard of by those
Full of loud intention and force.)

The secret life of growth is deaf to
The furious sound of demand,
And command, and all the other
Desperate hands of force racing
Circles and tensions, competing
To be the voices in charge of change
And future.
(While the future hides in the plain sight
Of a sweet revenge kept secret.)

Silent, I desire to comprehend the
Confidences of growth's habit and
Tells; to read the texts of life's future
That carry truth without provocation,
With signs as patient as the oldest secrets of life
Waiting for those willing to listen.

Colors and Light

if black is every color,
and white is every light.
is life every chance
for light
and color
to find the other truth of life?

Listen (Again)

When clouds part
              The sun shows
                           The eyes what

The soul knows

      The mouth shares
                  The words of
                         The new day.

                                    Who will listen?

The Sound of Freedom

What is the sound of freedom?
Song.
That's why they sing the songs of freedom.

What is the sound of freedom?
Song.
That's why they sing the songs of freedom.

What is the sound of freedom?
Song.
That's why they sing the songs of freedom.

What is the sound of freedom?
Song.
That's why they silence the songs of freedom.

These from the Jungle Shape

These from the jungle shape world as comes.
No privilege only verses of life and death.
Keep time on the tom-tom. Take speech as space.
There are demons and angels in the air we breathe.

Portly mother of worlds, so wild do you love
Your seeds with dream from vision through pain.
But you give only now, with the scent of a future
We could love if Time were persuaded to dance.

But these from the jungle shape world as comes.
Take time as it turns. Make life as it lives.

Tyranny Off Beat

proust called rhyme tyranny,
but tyranny is off beat
with the time of sound that
only the dancer knows
the key to making space out of myth.

can you see the future in the midst
like guerillas in the jungle, where
no curator can boutique or
ever link in their bio?

the revolution will not
be auto-suggested. i
will type out my own
message, and if i misspell
the prophecy or take
too much time,
i will call it slang,
or fashionably late.

can you not see that history
has gotten bored with
the same old shit. and
the same old shit is the
history of the off-beat
who can't keep up with
the new rhymes from the
future, which the tyrants
auto-correct.

Nubian and Nihil

"Naked woman, dark woman/Oil no breeze can ripple..."
                                                    -L.S. Senghor

I know a woman Nubian and nihil,
Strong in bone and flesh, with a luster
Held high in the wealth of a world
She houses alone. Her face is marble
And velvet, with brown eyes
And tears under her moonless skin
Drawn tight, drawn tight from the string
Of the bow she keeps in her fingers,
Daring to send a new world to flight.

She is Nubian and nihil, carrying
Every bone of her body with teeth
And state, consuming a desire of
Song lacking the luxury of a dancer.
When her eyes meet mine, I see a face
Full of self, commanding a spell
Of her bronze allure too comprehensive
For mere knowledge.

She is Nubian and nihil, the empress
Once of a sun dynastic, from which
The glare to behold her totality strikes
Proud eyes with repentance and the
Envy of a matchless power.
A crown of pure life—Black Athena!
On your throne shaping the wisdom
Of all intelligences and war.

Nubian and nihil. And still we fail
To catch your flight, until we see
The rich trails of your falling dusk reveal
Your existence, the knife edge of life.
Our last twilight, before the idols
Scatter our strength, and strain
Your vision to search for vows
That always vanish before the face
Of terror that remains the same.

But she is Nubian and nihil.
Our past and future right before us.
Our present event no god could ever make
From the rib of a sleeping man.
She is the woman who made the man
Awake to see the living gods,
From a conception truer than the immaculate.
Wake us up again to see anew.

She, Me, and da Vinci

There she is. Sitting, waiting,
                    wondering   if

The Mona Lisa
is only staring at her; while I watch,
                              wondering   if

She
is only waiting for me; while da Vinci somewhere
                              is waiting to see   if
We
are the only two in the world with time to wonder.

I consider approaching
          her; she considers approaching
          the Mona Lisa,
          da Vinci somewhere considers approaching
          us. But,

We all three halt.   We all three wait.   We all three wonder.

Can we afford to wonder with limited time?
Does wonder extend time beyond   limit?

76

The Last James Bond

"Poor fool, poor blind fool, I thought with sincere compassion,
mugged by an invisible man!" -Ralph Ellison, The Invisible Man

What if the last James Bond was black?
Not a double agent but a secret agent,
With a secret agency operating
Under his deference and reserve.
His master plan would be as discreet as the notch on
His lapels. He's on duty, and after intel,
Not the glamour or the fame they appoint
To him, because they find his speech eloquent,
And his cologne warm, and his distinction
The most interesting thing to regard of a black man.
He's after intel, and his speech is as
Doubled as his consciousness of the veil he plans
To cut up into a thousand pocket squares.
This is why his deference retains a pale mystery
To those who question the unnamed insecurity they
Feel between their knees, when he stands beside them
Fixed and aloof.

Time would be his ultimate refuge, since history
Made him an orphan of universality, and by that,
Made him the perfect man for the job.
He is the reason the subaltern will always speak.
His voice is in parentheses; thus, his weapon of choice is
A silencer, silent as the last star to appear at the gathering
Of the night. Always slept on.
That is why only the dreamer can blow his cover

And make a romance out of the conspiracy he keeps
Inside his shirtsleeves, while his target, who still believes
In a simple supremacy, plays the role of president
To the masses, as this secret agent man accepts
A vice invisibility, perfect for completing the finishing
Touches on his master plan without bother, using the
Lack of recognition to clothe his naked incognito, as he moves
Past the guards, walks down the sacred halls without urgency,
Playing in his head the music of the moment when
They will realize too late, that he has broken the code

To the safe, emptied the vault, escaped to an island
That was never supposed to exist, and now stands
Atop a world, with all he has brought from the bottom.
And the weary tears that can be seen for only a moment, before
The Merino wool of his suit absorbs their escape, is the only evidence
Of a mission impossible completed.

Husbandry of Forgotten Flowers

A father is first a husband.
And I don't mean a man who marries
A wife who dies when the scars of her body
Stop healing, and his heart needs so much love
To find the healing for his scars,
While his children wander distant.

I mean the husband who knew the seeds
That fell to the ground and found habit in the earth
Were his seeds, still rooted to him, still carrying
The evidence of his power to set out life, now left
To the chances of surviving a surrendered bed.
Left to the chances of surviving
The weeds and rot, the chances of
Surviving the crowding and the pestilence,
The chances of surviving the stones and disease,
Surviving the tread and the drought.
The chances of weakly breaking through
The surface and finding the face of an enormous sun,
The chances of daring to bear body and meager stalk,
Daring the chance to show foliage and flower.
Bearing flowers wild, lost, and free, daring
To stand up crooked and colorful, showing
Teeth to a world too busy to stop and read
The poetry of its survival, the poetry made from
The sun that caressed its ears with golden horns
Just as it is cut down and taken to give a
Pistachio green room an ironic accent.

A father is first a husband.
And I don't mean the man who marries
A wife who dies when the scars of her body
Stop healing, and his heart needs so much love
To find the healing for his scars,
While his children wander distant.

I mean the husband who must be reminded that
He has flowers he has forgotten,
Forgotten flowers barely surviving,
Forgotten flowers soon to give ironic accents
To so many pistachio green rooms.

The History of Black

The history of black
Is more than famous names and inventors;
More than the first or the greatest;
More than the king or the slave.

Learning the history of black
Is learning the history of faces without names,
Learning the history of bodies never understood,
It cannot fit in a month.

The history of black is the response of the soul
Clap; it is the vision of the black maybe; it is
The everyday move of the right on.

The history of black is the history of sound
Beyond a note. It is the history of calling
Beyond a speech. It is the history of revolution
Beyond a dream.
It cannot fit in a month.

The history of black is the blackness
Of history beyond erasure.
The history of belief beyond hope,
The history of joy beyond pain,
The history of us beyond them.

81

The history of black is the history
Of a world still beautiful despite history,
A world still beautiful beyond history,
A world still beautiful rewriting history.
It cannot fit in a month.

The Next Future May Be a Revenge Kept Secret

*"...the preservation of Black life is articulated in and with the
violence of innovation." -Fred Moten & Stefano Harney*

I did not come to cast a ballot but a cobra at your feet.
The leaders have failed to produce a world
We can survive, and the history they have used
To surround us is running out of time.
(And yet, they aren't running out of money.)

I turned my back to their audience like Miles
And played my song of broken words, spelling
Strategies for Tyree, Markeze, and Mikayla, to
Learn how to steal as much freedom as they can.
Because the next future may be a revenge kept secret.

How could you not understand that I am not
Your patriot, when your *patri* is not my *patri?*
I wasn't self-evident in "these truths" your fathers held,
And you are still holding on to "these truths" that
Erased my fathers.
The next future may be a revenge kept secret.

I will not carry the skin of my flesh like a wound
Or dress, or even a right to be justified by you as equal.
It is my only chance to feel the significance
Of being alive on a stage too short to run around in circles.
And the revolutions of your futures are circles of your
History preserved at the expense of the skin of my flesh.
The next future may be a revenge kept secret.

You have taken ownership of all the spaces, and now
You want to gentrify my time with your imperatives,
And corrections of what I need to know and need to do,
Because it concerns you that I choose to have the freedom
Of the flower no forest will ever own as known,
And my responsibility to your history waits on the
Power of the dancer who carries dreams in her legs,
And beats the ground with insurrection,
And at that point, the prayers for the music to adopt us
Are finally answered, while the desperation of a world
Bent on our submission turns to ashes in our hands.
The next future may be a revenge kept secret.

When the next future fully comes, it will be a revenge
Kept secret, like lovers eloping under ancient stars that
Must come down, stars that must fall from the sky
When the heights of the love-making bring every
Giant to kneel; forced to kneel in a
Repentance too expensive to be redeemed.
A repentance too late to matter.
The next future may be a revenge kept secret.

Beauty Alive is the Beast Undying

And I opened my eyes
And saw the beauty that was written
From the marks of the beast
Growing from the faces of sadness
And relentless music, caressing
These ones, marked with the colors of flesh
And blood darkened by the thick nectar
That fell from the opened sky,
Gathering together the young and the old,
The weak and the wise, all those
Made of fire and savannah,
Rising from the ashes of a history haunted,
A history valiant and beloved;
A history everywhere trapped
And still raging, still raging with the undying
Freedom and beauty of the beast that
Continues to consume the limits
Of its hunters, with nails biting
The palms of its clenched fists.

The World Black, Beautiful, and Beast

The beast is the pure showing of face,
Without the security of recognition
From the masters of indifference
And allergy, these ones incapable of beholding
Those monstrous eyes and glaring
Teeth that coruscate in the dark,
Carrying upon beleaguered bodies
Skin too maroon to be captured,
Even as the tremors surround the
Hills of its final stand.

Who will read these marks of the beast
Aloud with pride flaring in their nostrils,
As the noisy breathing of the survival
Camps under the powerful chin, and
Proclaim: See how this beast pulls in breath barely
Promised with jaws set and heart pounding!
See how this beast consumes cages!
See how this beast outlives history!
See how this beast keeps beauty from dying
In the murderous hands of those that fear freedom;
Those that fear the beautiful freedom of the
Undying beasts!

The Panther (Re: W. Blake)

"You tom-tom, tom-tom of the panther's pounce." -L.S. Senghor

Panther, panther burning black.
Of the jungle, labeled lack.
What allergic hand or eye
Prevents your ceaseless symmetry?

The wild of beauty you behold
In song: the timbres of the soul;
You cut the darkness with your eye
And styled a goddess of the sky.

The hammer and the chain were used
Against the mystery you produced
Before a hope in politics
Encaged your reasons to resist.

The diasporas of you prove
A metaphor too rich for truth
To wait on knowledge to divine
The liberties you shape of time.

Dispossessed of space beyond a reach
You made a *οὑτόπος* of speech.
They question your validity,
When from chains came originality.

Panther, panther burning black.
Of the jungle which you lack.
What immortal hand or eye
Could grasp your ceaseless symmetry?

Oil

I

oily yellows and tantrums of orange
revolving and sprawled along the horizons
of my earnest questions following the protests
and the promises and imperatives
all trending and hardly thought out

the lies of their truth shed light
on the proposition that shadows
are less honest than illusions,
even though they take their cues from the light.

II

so this is what sent 1,000 restless nights into philosophy?
since they deny desmond and me room in their inn,
i overlooked their loudly rolled-out salvation in a manger.
but professors of lies are a blur anyway
when you speed down the strip with the window
rolled down looking for a stony place
to lay your head under nights
that are insecure and usually deaf
to those who dream of ladders and future
while the dying stars of those jealous nights
are given no audience from weary dreamers.
and so they cry and wail and grow pale
and their pets chase their own tails
in pink circles of misrecognition.
how cute.

III

empty glasses remain filled with apparitions of tomorrow,
longing for a thirsty drink to pour across the parched tongue
tired of speaking prophesies in the wrong language all day.
i am sure you didn't know that whisky, when it is warm,
can hold prophecies in the back of a believing throat
for as long as is necessary.
try to consider the anxieties of these tomorrows
in the form of the protests of these today's
and you will see that history does in fact repeat itself,
first as farce and second as more farce.
But nobody's laughing.

IV

my eyes sometimes panic from what my mind does not fear
since i can see, under the giants' greedy gallop,
their cheap flaps, flapping and floundering,
flapping and floundering,
lacking the kind of irritation my age and time gathered
from claims and promises of justice and hope
with fancy, ambitious lies crafted by saints
dressed up as sinners thinking they were sinners
dressed up as saints to condemn the request
of Heriodias' daughter who could afford
those high prices while enjoying
complimentary prosecco before
the arrival of their silver platter of a prophet's head
who rejected the well-organized mother who planned
to turn the jungle into a nanny state of intentionality
and community-building
while running the last black man to think otherwise
off a cliff because he didn't read your recommendations,
just as you didn't read his recommendations.
so you pause for an awkward moment of silence
long enough to forget why
and return to the small talk of the old rich man
who would have given his children's inheritance
to the poor had he not become dumb of language from
getting rich in a land where sophistication is scandal
and sport is loyalty and love is a warm cloth
keeping nice truffles for so many cute pictures.
adorable.

92

V

coffee burns the tongue of the slow learner
dazzled by the regalia of his representative posing
furiously before a world removed from eyes and sensibility,
chasing loud mouths thirsty for oily sarcasm and correctness.
can you hear the torment? see the lines wrapping
around the building? the best fish and bread
offered entirely expensive, and the crowd
dines with laughter and selfies
desiring panna cotta and port after bellies
full of photogenic glories advocating
for those poor victims who had to make their claims
for justice in terms purely white and western
to men with strong calves who exercise
by practicing leaping over tall buildings
their fathers erected now redesigned
by their daughters with the latest fashion shown
in hurry and flashes and virals that disappear to give
space for more virals to disappear.
so relevant.

VI

do you think jerry springer would still
be willing to interview a room of naked
bodies running into walls padded with copious
amounts of pink, soft cotton made to look like
painful flesh so long as it proved to be therapeutic?
does the stench from a lie
delivered in the place of a kiss
that was intended to be an accident
by the fates give us any clue that
when you tell me that you love me
and i finish my breakfast and tell
you that gary coleman made me laugh
as a child but not cry when he died
since i am too old to remember
his face but only the character he played
that you and i need to sit down
and talk about what in the world
we really fear we can lose
in this life which if it went on
forever, we would die from
such a cruel embarrassment of time?

VII

i was getting off a plane in norway, marking places
i had never seen, read about, longed to walk
down its streets, and i am told a story that
those in love can find a pink sky that
pours certain rains able to fall directly into
smartly placed mason jars filled with frogs
that flood out and would, if they were blessed with the kind
of legs to do so, challenge giraffes to a staring contest
since whatever darling lovers can imagine
with their darling lovers' eyes can turn
the miracle of liberty into irony, but
a fearless page of questions beyond the recognition
of a darling care finds itself
still awaiting phrases for sentences,
and sentences for narratives,
and narratives for publishers,
and publishers for futures of colors unnamed
because color cannot be named.

VIII

i wonder if summer knew what i meant
the day she left me for good and forgot
to take the song i wrote her as a gift
i left on my glass table next to the bottle
of campari and cointreau and my tobacco,
while i sat in a pool of styrofoam
and milk, waiting for her as i chewed almonds
and recited a new song about running
for president in the first country
to draw its borders in crayola, flying
a flag of dreams and lipstick and praying
hands over spilled grenache. but she
never came back and since then
my mind has been running away
from the needs of my past as my hands
type words my understanding is too sure to
fear as incapable of achieving its
dream of the world and the baroque while lunging
at the face of cute laziness and indifference
taking the name of normal or busy
or confused or political
or one of those sham black faces
in high places mixing metaphors
of whiteness as a way to even the score
without the strength to end the game.
literal counterfeit white man.

IX

but what can i do when night after night
is houred with time trading wonders of
questions for answers and whispers of
calm and obligation and promises
to pay us back with a future from an empire
woke to the cutting-edge solutions designed
by smart young men and women
who tell stories of the ways
they rebuked old racists and perverts who
mistreated their victims and lied
about everything; these smart, affluent,
young men and women helplessly
chained, as well, to turquoise terrors of government,
now fume from the mouth to be
the loudest voice of the oppressed,
even as the tradition of advantage and wealth
stack behind them and their children
and they call this the guilt of privilege instead of the take of
the accomplice because they have determined
to turn the travesties into a triumphant unity
so the talk of the victor's generosity can
continue uninterrupted, and the sponsorships
for the victors to build communities can continue
uninterrupted, and the building of communities by the victims
can remain interrupted; which is all so basic, and just
as interesting as the ethics of the non-profiter,
which always reeked of double talk and burnt sage
and lives untouched by the burning heart of struggle

that knows the tired truth that fell asleep bored
behind the push of antsy revolutions sitting beside
orders of mussels and butter and merlot and trepidations
of the darker skin crawling along the floors
and up the legs of the table like cockroaches
after the basket of fries.

X

because all that is missing in the title is the "y."

C.I. Aki, the son of a Nigerian economist and a Nigerian-Jamaican horticulturalist, is a poet, essayist, filmmaker, and educator based in Nashville, Tennessee. He received his B.A. in Rhetoric and Sociology from the University of Texas at Austin and his Master's in Theology and Philosophy at Vanderbilt Divinity School. In 2012, he published his first short story, "A Withering Scar, a Thin Pin-Striped Suit, and 1,000 Judgments," in *34th Parallel Magazine*. In 2014, he premiered his short film, *The Runner*, in the Capital City Black Film Festival. In 2015, he was a recipient of Vanderbilt's Imagination Grant to carry out research in Spain for an on-going documentary on flamenco he is producing. He writes against the racialized misinterpretation of the achievement gap by education reform, and he currently leads a language arts program at an independent school in Nashville. When he is not writing or reading, he's working in his garden with a constant eye out for snakes.

Acknowledgments

This book would not be possible without the anxiety, anger, and joy shared with my family back home in Austin, Texas. Because of our pain and joy, I have these stories to tell. Additionally, I wouldn't have built on those stories without my Nashville day-ones from Vandy Div - Graham Scott and Desmond Coleman. Because of you two, I kept writing to outrun the erasure. On that note, I should thank that racist professor who made sure I wouldn't get into the Ph.D. program at Vandy – *Nemo me impune lacessit*. I am grateful for how things turned out.

However, I couldn't have completed these stories without the enduring ear of my fiancée, who listened to understand, knowing she could never fully understand. Thank you for trusting what makes me different.

Finally, this book wouldn't have happened without the fearless, eccentric eye of April Gloaming Publishing. You all are badass. Good looking out.